AF272957

Philip H. Pelly

A Last Goodbye?

novum ◢ pro

This book is also
available as
e-book.

www.novum-publishing.co.uk

© 2022 novum publishing

ISBN 978-3-99131-168-3
Editing: Hugo Chandler
Cover photos: Vchalup, Hdsidesign,
Kts, Kiosea39 | Dreamstime.com
Cover design, layout & typesetting:
novum publishing

www.novum-publishing.co.uk

CHAPTER ONE

In March 1918, at the age of nineteen, my father went off to fight in the trenches of the First World War. As a subaltern, he had a life expectancy of about six weeks. He took in his pocket a little prayer book into which his mother had inscribed in tiny meticulous handwriting Psalms 91 and 121: two of the loveliest poems extolling the power of God to protect us. I have held this prayer book in my hand and looked at it many times; it still brings tears to my eyes. Her desperate hope must have been that somehow God would protect him.

Volume three of "The Grenadier Guards in World War One" gives a written account of my father's regiment's exploits over the following months. It makes grim reading. A litany of woundings and deaths in the clipped dispassionate style of the time, with generally only the names of the officers being mentioned. I get the feeling that the deaths of the other ranks were not deemed to be so important, or maybe they were just too numerous to be named. No regrets: not sons or fathers or husbands, but pawns on an unending chessboard where the only rule was to do one's duty.

It was several months later, in September, in a charge against the enemy line, that my father was struck by a bullet in his chest. He told me that as he lay on the ground his only concern was that people would think he was malingering, funking the rest of the charge. Fear of the shame of not doing one's duty exceeded any fear of death. The bullet passed through his torso and exited at the back, doing no serious damage to his internal organs. It was a lucky bullet, taking him out of the remainder of the war.

Which is as good a place as any to start this little book. For it concerns death, the fear of death, and the sadness it causes. I have reached an age when it is certainly starkly apparent that there is a lot more runway behind me than in front. My aim in writing my reflections on this is to try to bring some comfort and hope – primarily to people who have reached the same stage in their lives. But it is also for anyone who may be interested in whether at the end of our days on earth we snuff out into oblivion or whether we take off into an entirely new existence of life after death. No one can know for sure, and I do not flatter myself that I can persuade anyone to the high degree of probability with which I hold my belief that we take the latter course. But I do hope that I can help people at least to consider that possibility to be a realistic one. That we and our loved ones may go on to beat death, that there will be no final goodbyes.

We are so certain of things nowadays. No more mysteries, no more wonders. With the click of a mouse, no more not knowing the answers to anything we want to know. We are not used to uncertainties. Apart from our prejudices, we like to have facts which can be proved. We view with amused contempt the superstitions of the past, the egotistical gods of the Greeks and Romans and all those terrifying ancient gods, including the Sun God of the Aztecs who would not rise in the morning without human sacrifice. How we ridicule the old belief that the Earth was flat, and that the Earth was the centre of the universe and that anyone who dared say otherwise deserved to be put to death for blasphemy. Such ignorance. And yet people were no less clever then than they are now. They just knew less about things.

So, what have we got to be so proud of? Here we are, little specks of life stuck by gravity to the spinning ball of the Earth rotating around our Sun. One Sun among maybe two hundred billion or so other suns in our galaxy. One galaxy among maybe one hundred billion or so other galaxies in the Universe. So at least we now know our place in the grand scheme of things, and perhaps we can be proud of that.

Or do we? The trouble is that there is approximately ninety-five percent of the Universe that we know virtually nothing about. We can calculate that it is there, but we don't know what it is made of, and we can't even see it. For that reason, it is called Dark Matter and Dark Energy. So, the truth is, the things we actually know about are limited to five percent of all that exists inside us and around us and out there in the furthermost reaches of the Universe, including all those mind-boggling numbers of suns and galaxies. Metaphorically perhaps we are not so very different to those flat earth people, happy in their exalted position at the centre of the Universe. We think we know it all. But clearly we do not.

Consequently, my hope in writing this book is to persuade those sceptical of the existence of life after death that if they are basing their scepticism on scientific or other logic, this basis may be rather suspect. As with a flat earth person trying to argue that life could not exist on the underside of the earth because anything there would fall off, so too it might seem rather futile for someone to argue, based on their experience of only five percent of all that exists, that something else does not exist. Furthermore, our understanding of that five percent is in any event very far from complete.

I find that many people are happier talking about the possibility of some sort of a vague, divine power existing than they are in talking about the possibility specifically of God's existence. They are content for an unspecified supernatural power to remain buried in the background of their lives as long as it is never allowed out into the foreground. It seems to me that life after death is unlikely without the existence of a divine power which transcends our earthly laws to enable this. What I am discussing here is the God whom I believe to exist, a God who set off the Big Bang nearly fourteen billion years ago and who planted the seeds of our existence when the Earth was formed over four billion years ago. The God I have in mind is so extraordinary that it is not surprising that so many people do not believe in him. This is an all-powerful God who created the Universe, and us, and who provides us with freedom of will and with life after death. This is a God of infinite love and compassion, in common with the beliefs of all the major Abrahamic based faiths. Tempting as it may be to turn one's back on such a disturbing, mind-bending concept and concentrate instead on what we consider to be the important issues in our worldly lives, if such an all-powerful God does exist, it might be argued that it would perhaps be unwise to ignore him.

Of course, my belief is no more than belief, without proof or provable fact. Why then, you may ask, does an ordinary worldly sort of person such as I consider myself to be, not much given to wishful thinking, hold it? What a curious, anachronistic, perhaps even crazy thing to do, you may think. So let me try to explain.

I accept that my belief was initiated and largely dictated by my upbringing and culture. My parents were conventional Christians. They survived hard, cruel times. My mother was too young to take any part in the war effort. But she was not immune to the harsh brutalities of life in those days. She told me how she remembered seeing the bodies of dead children, I assume victims of the Spanish flu, being trundled away in wheelbarrows for burial. That made a lasting impression on her, and she never stopped worrying about the safety of her own children. My father was rather the opposite. Having survived the horrors of the trenches and then, in the Second World War, having survived the blitz as a firewatcher stationed at the top of St Paul's Cathedral, I think he understandably took a somewhat relaxed view about any perils that might arise in peacetime.

Before and during the Second World War, my five siblings were born. I was born three years after the war. Shortly after that we all moved from London to a large and glorious old rectory in the beautiful village of Grittleton in Wiltshire. So far as I can remember, we went to church most Sundays. I can't say that I took any interest in the services, other than when they would finish. The vicar was a kindly old chap, so kind that although he smoked a pipe (Three Nuns tobacco I believe) he always carried a well-stocked cigarette case to offer round. When I was about three or four years old he came to tea and produced the cigarette case. It must have caught my attention, because for some reason he told me that if I could work out how to open it then I could have one of the contents.

It didn't take me long. Surprised and, since this took place in front of my parents, probably rather embarrassed, as a man of the cloth he obviously felt duty-bound to honour his offer. I seem to remember that my father expressed the pragmatic view that smoking a cigarette would make me sick and put me off smoking for life. Regrettably, he was wrong. I am ashamed to say that from then on whenever the coast was clear my little fingers would remove a cigarette from my father's gold cigarette case and take it, together with a borrowed box of Swan Vesta matches, to the potting shed. There I would luxuriate in the pungent smoke from the struck match and then deliciously inhale the cigarette smoke.

That was the first time that my life was influenced by a priest in the Church of England. It was also the last for many years.

It was probably about this time that my father became a Lay Reader in the Church. Lay Readers are now known as Licensed Lay Ministers, and usually have to undergo several years training before being appointed. My father was rather proud of the fact that all he had to do was to have tea with the Bishop. In fact, however, I have no doubt that he already had a profound knowledge of the Bible and a very deep faith – which must have been apparent to the Bishop. I suppose that this must, in a small way, have been apparent to me even as a very young child. Every night, he would settle me down as I lay in bed with a hymn which he would sing to me and a prayer which we would say together. His unwavering faith must have had a huge influence on my unquestioning infant mind.

My father's Lay Readership gave rise to a bit of a coincidence in my life. One afternoon when I was about five, the Rural Dean, Canon Daniel Anthony, and his wife came to tea. Tea must have loomed large in the Church of England in those days, and this must have been a particularly important one. I seem to remember that my ten-year-old brother Roland and I were sent outside to enable the grown-ups to have some peace. The Old Rectory had a large circular drive in front of it and a lane to the side, which passed the garage and led onto the field beyond. This had enabled my father to teach Roland how to drive his Ford Consul. So, with nothing better to do, Roland collected the car key, and we went for a joy ride round and round the circular drive. When we had had enough, Roland brought the trip to a grand finale by showing off his driving prowess by coming up fast behind the Canon's car parked outside the front door and jamming on the brakes at the last moment.

Perhaps his prowess was not as high as he had thought, or perhaps it was the loose gravel surface of the drive. Whatever it was, we smashed rather forcibly into the rear of the Canon's car. The good Canon was presumably somewhat taken aback when my ten-year-old brother sheepishly confessed that he had driven into the back of his car, but he took it in good spirit. It was a fine example of Christian forgiveness. I don't think that he ever came to tea again, though.

The coincidence was that about sixteen years later, sadly after Canon Anthony had died, Mrs Anthony came to tea again, this time to discuss my engagement to her daughter. With hindsight, I suspect that she had misgivings about her daughter marrying into a family which contained feral ten-year-old children who were allowed manically to speed around in their father's car and crash into things. I think it had taken her some time to come round to the view that my family was not quite such a bad lot as Roland's infant driving had led her to believe.

I started my education at a girls' school just across the road from the Old Rectory. It was a rambling old place which took very young boys until they were old enough to go to prep school. There, we were taught scripture sanitised from most of the unpleasant bits of the Bible. There were prayers every morning and always a faint fear of doing something wrong and being sent to the rather formidable head mistress. I don't think I ever quite knew what corrective measures the head mistress would take if the occasion arose; fortunately, it never did. But I think I assumed that it would involve a slipper.

There were never many doubts about what happened to transgressors at the Gloucestershire Prep Boarding School to which I next went. At the conclusion of morning prayers, the head master would read out a list of the names of the boys who were to see him in his study straight away. I seem to remember that this was a frequent occurrence and that there was usually a boy or boys who would slink out after prayers with a red face and drooping shoulders. The only doubt was which cane he would use. He had a variety of these on display in an umbrella stand in the hall, ranging from a thin whippy one to a thick nobly one reserved for the worst offenders. You never really knew whether your name would be on the list because you lived in constant fear that you might have done something judged to be wrong without even knowing it. I can't say that the shadow of this usual conclusion to prayers enhanced my devotions.

Some of the masters were decent and humane. Most of them were not. The bad ones were distinguished one from another by their inclination and ability to inflict fear and pain on us. The head master was not the only one to use a cane, and those who did all had different techniques, some more dreaded than others. One of the masters had perfected a way of pulling boys' hair in a particularly unpleasant way. Another had a solid glass rod which he used to hit us on the head with, until the day came when he hit one boy so hard that it broke. One of the masters was reputed to have been a spy in the war. He was a morose, uncommunicative person – I don't think that I ever saw him smile. He didn't resort to violence; he didn't have to. If you fell foul of him, he would threaten to stand you in the corner until you had learnt the Bible "from cover to cover". He was such a cold, sinister individual that we believed him. Perhaps not the best of ways to engender affection for the word of God.

The school holidays were, however, wonderful. Grittleton was a lovely place in which to grow up. It had a village shop owned by an obliging middle-aged lady, Mrs Abrahams, who was always happy to believe me when I told her that the packets of ten Woodbines I would scrape my pocket money together to buy were for my father. In those days there was a legal minimum age of sixteen years old for buying cigarettes, and I was several years below that. She seemed to forget that when my father bought cigarettes for himself, they were always the more expensive Piccadilly's in packets of twenty.

There was a post office to which I was sometimes sent to purchase dog licences for seven shillings and sixpence, and well-thumbed stamps which in those days you had to lick to make them stick. There was a village school run by Mrs Marsden who was reputed to be very strict. There was a forge owned by the blacksmith Bill Wilkins, who was always happy to let us children watch him at work as he swished air into his flaming coals with huge overhead bellows and hammered into shape white and red-hot iron on his anvil. Sometimes a horse would come in to be re-shod. He always seemed to be happy, and there would always be a tuneless humming on his lips as he went about his work. One year I asked him to make a machine for me. I didn't say what sort of a machine; indeed, I had no idea myself what sort of a machine I wanted, and we never discussed how it would be paid for. Every now and again I would pop in to see him to ask how the machine was coming on. And every time with great patience he would find something to say to humour me.

There was the village pub, The Neeld Arms, which in later years I came to frequent with enthusiasm. But in those childhood years I kept clear of it. Drinking went on late into the night and the landlord was always hung over and in a bad mood the next day, with no patience for pesky children.

About half a mile from the Old Rectory was Dunley Wood, a lovely place in which to play. It had a rough track running through its centre, which boasted a rather fine brickwork bridge where it crossed a hollow in the topography. In the side of the hollow was an old brick-lined tunnel which Roland and I eventually found well-concealed under brambles. Of course, we had to walk through it, not a little concerned that it might collapse at any moment. It was reputed to have been built by one of the squires to save him from the sight of his workers, who were required to shuffle down it bent double while he drove grandly along the track in his carriage.

There were characters I will never forget. The carpenter whose workshop floor was always ankle deep in wood shavings and whose lips never without the last gasp of a roll-up, usually gone out. I don't remember ever seeing him doing much carpentry. But he was happy to let us children watch him at work which, so far as I can remember, mostly consisted of boiling up a pot of fish glue in preparation for whatever woodwork he might be called upon to do.

There was Vic Cole who, every year a few days before Christmas, would turn up at the back door with a conspiratorial look and a Christmas tree under his arm. Every Christmas I worried that he might forget, but he never did. My father never forgot to have a bottle of whisky ready to complete the transaction.

There was Edward, a Spaniard who had been on the side of the revolutionaries in the Spanish uprising against Franco. He had married one of the ladies in the village – I have no idea how they met. He was a very jolly, entertaining man, though he had a bit of a hunted look about him … I think that he always expected Franco's men to turn up and get him. But he was ready, for somehow he had managed to smuggle out of Spain a semi-automatic pistol which he proudly showed to my brother Antony, who used to engage him in long conversations about his exploits. Fortunately, Franco's men never came, and there were no gunfights in Grittleton.

In the churchyard, there was the grave of James the Apostle, which I discovered when I was about six or seven. I asked my parents why this saint should be buried in our churchyard, but they never seemed to understand what I was talking about. I was greatly intrigued by this until my reading improved and I saw that this was really the grave of one James Allpass.

So, no spill-over from the Spanish civil war and no saints. A typical village in the nineteen fifties (apart perhaps from Edward); rich or poor, everyone seemingly content. The rich, I suspect, rather more so. Undoubtedly an important part of society then was the church, and even though many people had little interest or understanding of what it was really all about, they wanted their baptisms, weddings and funerals to be conducted in the church. Generally, the clergy were respected and trusted as pillars of society, and I suppose that most people had some sort of a belief in God, if only by default. That's how it was, and that was my understanding of society.

School holidays, however, always came to an end. The unhappy day inevitably arrived when, sandwiched between my mother and father on the front bench seat of the Ford Consul, I would be taken back to prep school for the heart-sinking first day of term. Back to all those familiar smells and sounds, joining in the stiff-upper-lip false jollity with the other boys.

I remained a pupil of that school for about four miserable, homesick years. But there was one gloriously happy day. It was the day when the headmaster called in my parents and told them that they were wasting their money on my school fees; that I was so stupid that I would never get in to public school (for which his school was supposed to be preparing me); and that they may as well remove me forthwith and put me in one of those state schools which were good at training boys to do woodwork and metalwork and "things with their hands". By his standards, if you hated Latin, were no good at sports and were bad at spelling, you were a failure, fit only to be educated within the ranks of the lower orders. An ability to do science, such as it was in that school, and maths was completely irrelevant.

I suppose that the headmaster considered that his was a Christian school. I can't say that I ever saw much sign of it.

I can't remember whether I thanked God for my release from that cold, mean-spirited place. If I didn't I should have done.

By passing an informal exam which consisted mainly of maths questions, I was given a place in a boys' secondary technical school in the City of Bath. My father would drive me to the local train station in Chippenham, from where I would take a steam train to Bath every day. The school was a revelation in how a school should be. I did stand out as being "posh", but for the most part the other boys were forgiving of that and were curious as to why I was there, rather than antagonistic. The school had laboratories for science and proper teachers who could teach without intimidation. Discipline was strict but fair. There were the legally required communal prayers every morning led by the deputy head who seemed sincere in what he was doing. I don't think, however, that they strengthened any belief I had in God. But I suppose that they did engender a feeling that belief in God was part of the fabric of society.

I was allowed to take sandwiches and a Thermos of coffee for lunch: no longer did I have to struggle through disgusting plates of boiled swede and cold poached eggs. And joy of joys, I soon realised that by locking myself in the lavatory of the train I could have a peaceful cigarette on route to school and on the way back. As I got older and bolder, I would light up a pipe instead. For the first time I discovered that school could be really quite tolerable.

Distressingly, by now my mother had started to suffer from excruciatingly painful osteoarthritis. She consulted various doctors but none of them seemed able to help her. No doubt desperate for relief from the pain she eventually went to see a spiritual healer, Mrs Butterfield, who lived in a little house in Chippenham. She went to see Mrs B, as we came to call her, many times, and I accompanied her on some of those visits since I had become interested in the subject of spiritualism. Sadly, Mrs B was never able to bring about a cure for my mother, but she did relieve some of the pain, which was why she kept going to see her.

Mrs B was an extraordinary woman. Of course, there are some people who think that all spiritualists are fraudsters, out for the money. But Mrs B never charged for anything: the furthest she went in that direction was to invite people, if they wished, to put some money on a plate for her local Spiritualist Church, just as congregations in the Church of England are invited to do. Maybe I was young and impressionable, but even with the benefit of lots of cynical world-weary hindsight I can say that Mrs B was totally genuine, and one of the most sincere Christians I have had the privilege to know.

Mrs B was the leader of her church in Chippenham. I went to a few of her services which contained Bible readings and prayers, followed by a session with a medium who would endeavour to pass on messages from the dead to their grieving relatives and friends. A cynic might say that it was all a bit trivial and completely open to fakery. Of course, it was open to fakery, but it does not necessarily follow that it was fake, and the messages certainly did seem to help and comfort their recipients.

The best medium of all, however, was Mrs B herself. I anticipate that the eyes of even the most loyal of readers are beginning to roll but bear with me. I was lucky enough to have several conversations with her on a one-to-one basis, and they were fascinating. She told me of her understanding of the afterlife about which she had no doubt, and she had messages for me which I am afraid I have mostly forgotten but which meant a great deal to me at the time.

There was one message which I do clearly remember, which seemed completely implausible. It was that sometime in the future I would work to help children. My only ambition at that time was to become a scientist; I had no thoughts whatsoever of working with children or having anything to do with children apart, perhaps, in due course from having some of my own. The concept that a prediction could be made as to my future didn't surprise me. Mrs B was part of such an extraordinary world that pretty well anything seemed to be possible with her. But surely there was no possibility of such a prediction coming true? I will explain later why I believe that it did.

For those who may be thinking that I am completely unhinged for believing in the supernatural even after three score years and ten during which I should have learnt better, let me explain why I see no reason why I should not do so. Putting it quite simply, there is nothing odder about the supernatural things that we don't really understand than there is about the weird counter-intuitive realm of quantum physics that we don't really understand.

The same, in my view, goes for belief in God. People say that there is no place for God in this modern scientific era. We have, they say, science to answer our questions. They feel confident enough to say that, even though science at the moment knows in detail only about five percent of all the stuff in the universe, with the rest remaining dark to us. I don't seek in any way to suggest that the answers to theological questions lie in that darkness, I am merely pointing out that we are very far from knowing it all. When we come to consider what we do know we find that, within the realms of quantum physics, there are some very strange phenomena which in my view are just as strange as the concept of God. There is nothing unusual about strange and counter-intuitive things in nature; many such things do exist, and we have no alternative but to accept them.

In the next chapter I will briefly mention some of those phenomena. For the moment let me return to my school days and beyond.

I spent three relatively happy years at the Bath Technical School. But, by the age of fourteen, I was finding the constraints of school life, and being treated like a child, to be a little tedious. The opportunity arose for me to go to a college of further education in Chippenham and I leapt at the chance.

The North West Wiltshire Area College of Further Education was marvellous. There were no rules to speak of. I could smoke my pipe openly. No one bossed you about. There was no homework. You could come and go as you pleased. All you had to do was pass your exams. Despite being rather lazy I managed to do that, picking up some O levels and then A levels in maths, physics and chemistry. Best of all, it was there that I met the young woman who was later to become my wife.

My A level grades were sufficient to take me to London University to study physics. To my shame I was abominably lazy there, and I still have nightmares about the lectures I skipped and how little work I did. In the event, I was lucky to end up with a third-class honours degree in physics, which my brother Roland unkindly but accurately described as a boozer's degree. I had hoped to go on to take a Masters, but my degree wasn't good enough to get funding for that and so instead I took a Diploma in Education and then spent the next two years teaching.

Two years teaching was enough. I had married Helen on the conclusion of my degree, and her job as a legal executive gave me a glimpse into the workings of the law. A career in the law seemed much more attractive than my previous one. Thus it was that I decided to drop out into the law. In those days you could study for all the solicitors' qualifying exams by correspondence course, and you could do that at the same time as serving your articles (now known as a training contract). The laws of man were considerably easier to understand than the laws of physics, but they were a devil of a lot of hard work to memorise. I like to think that went some way to atone for my laziness in my previous studies. Three years later, much to my relief, I was admitted as a solicitor of the Supreme Court of Judicature, as it was grandly called.

So, from finishing A levels up until this point, not much God had been in my thoughts. I was too busy on other things. I think that it was probably the birth of my daughter and later my son that was the catalyst for me to look again at the deeper questions in life. Also, Helen had started to attend the local church fairly frequently and she sometimes managed to drag me along with her. The vicar was a rather crazy and very likeable fellow cutting an unusual dash in his top hat and flowing ecclesiastical cloak. He was impressively sincere in his faith, and I suppose it was the combination of that, together with the gratitude and joy of being blessed with two of the loveliest children that any parent could ever hope for, that made me turn again to consider whether God was behind it all.

In 1981 we moved to an old run-down farmhouse in a nearby village. The vicar, the Reverend Rodney Pope, had goodness written through him to his very core. As a young man he had served in Bomber Command in the Second World War, and together with the rest of his crew he had volunteered for a second tour of duty on conclusion of, and having survived, the first. Air crew didn't have to expose themselves to the enormous dangers of a second tour; it was a tremendously courageous thing to do.

Rodney had been trained to take the controls and do his best to land the aircraft in the event that the pilot was killed. But his main task was to aim the bombs, sighting them on the targets to be destroyed. He was deeply proud of his and his crew's wartime duty, but surely agonisingly conflicted as the Christian priest which he later became by the inescapable reality of the many people he had been involved in killing. I cannot say to what extent the friction of those two bedrocks of his psyche grinding together forged the man he was, but he was certainly the kindest and most humble man you could ever hope to meet, forgiving of others even if he could not quite forgive himself. He was one of those rare people whose example said it all. You knew that such a man had to be on the right track, that whatever belief inspired and drove him had to be good. His devout Christian convictions gave me a further gentle but firm push towards considering the enigma of God.

The impetus for me to find answers became more focused when Helen began the process of training to become a lay minister in the church. Often our conversations tended to be directed towards the affairs of God when I could bounce questions off her. After five years she completed her training and was licensed as a lay minister. As she became ever more involved in church affairs, I became ever busier as a litigation solicitor. My professional duty to bite metaphorical chunks out of my clients' opponents did rather conflict with the Christian duty to love one's neighbours, and neighbours had to take second place. Nonetheless, I had various personal experiences, which I will return to later, which increasingly persuaded me that the God as revealed by Jesus Christ really does exist.

After twenty years in the cut and thrust of private practice I was appointed as a district judge. It was wonderful to be relieved of the task of persuading others to make what I considered to be the right decisions and to be in a position to make them myself. Increasingly my work as a judge involved cases concerning children: disputes between parents, and sometimes grandparents, mostly over contact and residence. It was the most emotionally difficult and sometimes harrowing work I had ever done, and also the most fulfilling. And, of course, it reminded me of that prediction long before that I would work to help children. I am sure that I didn't always get it right. But I hope that for the most part I did secure good outcomes, or anyway the least bad outcomes, for the children involved in the usually bitter disputes I had to deal with.

In the meantime, Helen trained for and became licensed as a priest in the Church of England. So now I have direct access to a greatly loved priest for all my questions. If anyone had told us when we were courting, she with her ambitions in the law and me with my ambitions in physics, that one day she would be a priest and I would be a judge, we would have dismissed that out of hand. Such are the vicissitudes of life.

And such is the background which led me towards where I am now. Curious perhaps that I should think that I can help others facing the not very distant death of themselves or their loved ones. I have no theological qualifications or expertise. I am just an ordinary sort of person hoping to reach out to other ordinary people. I am not enrobed in religious ideals or dogma. I hope that I can show that none of that stuff is necessary to hold a belief in God and in the life hereafter which he promises us. At least, I hope that I can show that the presence of God and life beyond the grave is a realistic possibility. At the very least, that there is hope that they exist.

CHAPTER TWO

So, what about those strange phenomena of quantum physics which I referred to earlier? Through looking at what we can learn from these scientific phenomena, I hope to demonstrate that we should keep our minds as open about the existence of God and life after death as we have to do about the extraordinary things going on under our noses in science. I appreciate that not everyone has a great affection for science, and some people may find a chapter on quantum physics rather unappealing. I hope that I will be able to persuade you otherwise. The concepts are as weird as anything you can imagine, and so they are a little hard to take on board for the first time. But there is no need to struggle to understand why they are as they are because, so far as I am aware, no one understands that. If I fail to inspire you that will be my fault, not yours. And for those who really feel that they would rather not stomach it I will set out in the last three paragraphs of the chapter the main conclusions which emerge.

Before I begin, I should point out that it is over fifty years since I took my degree in physics. Not only am I extremely rusty on the subject, but there have been developments since then. I have had to try to lubricate those long inactive scientific cogs within my brain with a good deal of reading to update myself. So, some of the more recent stuff which follows may be almost as new to me as it is to you. We travel together.

Quantum physics is the science of tiny objects such as atoms, electrons and photons and many others. At this level of minuteness, very strange things happen which are often counter-intuitive and unlike anything that we are used to in everyday life on the macroscopic level. It is called "quantum physics" because in the early days over a hundred years ago when it was being developed, it was discovered that, down at this level, particles in matter are only allowed to exist at certain fixed levels of energy, or "quanta".

Light is a form of wave, in many ways similar to waves on the surface of the sea, (although unlike the sea, light waves do not need a medium such as water to move through: they will happily travel through a vacuum).The colour of the light is determined by the number of times the wave goes up and down per second, which is what is known as its frequency. The energy in the wave is directly proportional to its frequency. If two identical waves bump into each other then they will interfere with each other, so that if two crests converge they will form one bigger crest, and if two troughs converge they will form one bigger trough. If a trough and a crest converge they will cancel each other out; if they are water waves then the surface of the water will go flat and if they are light waves there will be darkness where the troughs and crests converge. This phenomenon of interference is a very good way of proving that light is indeed a wave.

Leaving light for the moment we will now move on to atoms. Atoms are the basic building blocks of matter, the smallest little whole bit that you can get of any element. Atoms are themselves made up of particles, so for example if we look at the simplest atom, that of hydrogen, it contains a nucleus which is a proton with a positive charge, and an electron which has an equal but opposite negative charge. The next simplest atom, that of helium, contains a bigger nucleus which has two protons (and two neutrons) and two electrons. And so it goes on from element to element, the nuclei getting bigger and carrying more positive charges with correspondingly more electrons with negative, but in total equal, opposite charges.

If it's that simple, you may be wondering, why are quantum physicists thought to be so clever? Well, actually it is very much more complicated than that, but I won't need to go into the complications save to say that it so happens that the electrons can only occupy certain permitted energy levels within the atom. They can, however, hop from one energy level to another. If an electron hops from a higher to a lower energy level it needs to get rid of the surplus energy which it does by emitting a quantum of electromagnetic radiation, for instance light. Electrons can also go the other way, going from lower to higher energy levels by, for instance, absorbing exactly the right amount of energy from the light. They can get so excited that they leave the atom altogether. Thus, if light is shone onto metal, electrons may be emitted from the surface (this is known as the photoelectric effect). It is found that the energy of an emitted electron is always the same for light of a given frequency (or colour).

The point to be drawn from this is that light comes in little packets of energy. Each packet gives up all its energy, which needs to be exactly the right amount, to the electron. These packets of energy behave as if they are particles, and one can therefore also consider light to be a stream of particles. The packets of energy are known as 'photons', and the amount of energy each contains is known as a 'quantum'.

We thus have to arrive at the curious conclusion that light is both a wave and a stream of particles (or even an individual particle if it is at its lowest intensity). This is known as 'wave-particle' duality. We know that light is a wave from the way that we have interference when identical waves collide. We know that it consists of particles from the photoelectric effect. Indeed, further supporting evidence for this can be found in other experiments which I need not go into here.

We get the same sort of effect with electrons. Electrons certainly are particles (a flow of electrons through a metal or gas constitutes an electric current). However, they can also behave as waves, and accordingly they too can exhibit interference. Their wavelength is shorter than visible light. This means, for instance, that they can be used in electron microscopes for giving better definition of tiny objects. Of perhaps even greater importance, quantum physicists would tell you that the atom as we know it could not exist if electrons did not behave as standing waves, not particles, when inside the atom.

So how can this be? How can light, and the electron, be both a wave and a particle at the same time? So far as I am aware, no one knows.

In fact, it is thought that all particles, not just electrons, have wave-particle duality, or would do so if this could be measured.

Human logic would say that such a thing is not possible. But human logic is clearly not always infallible and meets its match when it comes to certain aspects of quantum physics. Why should it be supposed that it is any less fallible when it comes to consider the strangeness of God, if he exists?

I am conscious that readers of a certain age may be puzzled by my reference above to electrons behaving as waves, not particles, when inside the atom. They may vaguely recollect long distant lessons when they were taught that atoms consist of a nucleus with electrons rotating around the nucleus, like the planets in the solar system rotate around the sun. It was a theory which seemed to fit so well, with the positive nucleus attracting the negative electrons, that attractive force being the centripetal force necessary to hold them in orbit.

But there was always a huge flaw in that theory, because whenever an electron is accelerated it gives off electromagnetic radiation. (This is, for instance, why a radio transmitting aerial works.). An electron spinning around a nucleus would effectively always be being accelerated towards the nucleus, and therefore would be losing energy in doing so. The effect of that would be that the electron would rotate more and more slowly and then crash into the nucleus, causing the atom to collapse. This, of course, does not happen. If it did, life as we know it would not exist.

However, if one considers an electron in an atom to be a standing wave, rather like a standing wave vibrating on the string of a musical instrument, then there is no problem. The atom does not collapse, and just as the string of a fixed length in a musical instrument can vibrate at only certain frequencies, the electron can possess only certain levels of energy which is, of course, exactly what one finds to be the case.

Permit me to digress a little at this stage to point to something of a parallel in ordinary life: in this case, in judicial life. When I was a newly appointed deputy district judge and learning the ropes, I used to sit at the same court as a very experienced judge whom I shall call Harry. Harry was coming up to seventy years old and was much respected and rather feared by many of the advocates who appeared before him. He had a deep, fruity, authoritative, almost Churchillian, voice and a stern look about him that few people argued with. Solidly middle class, you would say. Yet in one of our first conversations over lunch he told me with great pride that his father had been a labourer. He told me how he had come up the hard way. No university for him. He had passed his solicitors qualifying exams and served his articles with a snooty city firm of solicitors. When he thought the time was right he had suggested to this firm that they might like to take him on as a partner. The response was that they only ever took on partners who had been to public school. No matter how good a solicitor he might be, that would not be good enough.

Harry still felt aggrieved about that several decades later, but he had obviously taken it on the chin at the time, as he went off and joined another firm where he made good, and eventually got elevated to the bench. I think he felt justifiably proud about that. But he never forgot his roots, and his first advice to me was that one should always remember with everyone in distress such as facing possession of their homes for non-payment of rent or mortgage that "there but for the grace of God go I". That was probably the wisest advice that I ever had about how to be a judge.

Harry loved to tell the story of how once he had been returning to the court building after lunch. He came to the entrance glass swing doors and noticed a man on the other side who he assumed was respectfully waiting for him to pass through first. Surely everyone knew that he was the judge. So Harry pressed on through. But the man did not realise that Harry was the judge, and shoved Harry out of the way with the immortal words: "Get out of my way you fat little f...er".

Harry's displeasure was not to fester for long. A few minutes later, Harry's afternoon case, a matrimonial dispute, was called in. His joy was unbounded when he saw that the husband was the man whom he had met at the swing door. With great propriety he announced that the respondent husband had been extremely rude to him outside, relating precisely what he had said. Imagine Harry's inner delight when he informed the husband that had he behaved that way in court he would already be halfway to Chelmsford prison. This of course meant that Harry could not possibly proceed with the case since he could no longer be seen to be impartial. So, he adjourned the case, recusing himself and ordering the (probably by now horrified) husband to pay all the wasted costs of the adjournment. The fact that Harry would not now have to hear another tedious matrimonial dispute that afternoon and could instead catch up on his paperwork was an added bonus.

Harry actually regarded the saga as wonderfully amusing, even though the husband's two adjectives were plainly accurate. So, as with those quantum particles, Harry was two things at once, the stern rather formidable judge which he certainly was, but also a self-deprecating man with a heart of gold and unbridled sense of humour. Probably rather a tenuous illustration I know, but I couldn't resist mentioning Harry's story!

Let us return to the God question. I suspect that for many of us the concept of an all-powerful God creating the universe and everything in it, including us, is so unlike anything we encounter anywhere else, so alien to normal existence, so impossible to understand, that it has no meaning for us. And how can anything so fundamentally meaningless have any interest for us?

One answer to that may lie in Copenhagen. Let me explain.

We look again to light waves interfering with one another. One way of demonstrating interference (first carried out in 1799) is to prepare a piece of card with two minutely narrow parallel slits close together cut in it. The card is stood up vertically. A beam of light is then aimed at the two slits so as to allow part of it to pass through the slits and onto a screen behind. If the slits are narrow enough, the light passing through them will, on emerging, fan out so that a new wave front is created at each slit. Since they originally came from the same source the two new waves will be identical (in phase with each other) and as they spread out into each other they will interfere. If you look at the screen you will see bright bands where the crests or troughs of the waves combine and dark bands where the crests and troughs cancel each other out.

With the benefit of more modern technology, it is possible to reduce the intensity of the beam of light so that it consists of just one photon at a time (light being both photons and waves). One might expect that each individual photon (being a particle) would pass through one or other of the slits, and therefore that there could no longer be any interference. If the screen is replaced by a photographic film, and if one carries on letting through one photon at a time each photon will make a pinprick of light on the film. However, if a large number of photons is allowed to pass through one at a time, one will find that, contrary to expectation, there will be a pattern of light and dark bands recorded on the photographic film which is the same as the pattern on the screen when the intensity of the light is not restricted. Although the track of each individual photon is random, the light bands are where the individual photons congregate, and the dark bands are where no photons arrive on the film. Letting through photons one by one for a long time gives the same effect as letting through lots of photons for a short time.

But how can it be that one photon at a time can interfere? How can it interfere with itself? Perhaps, somehow, it separates and passes through both slits together, although it seems unlikely that a photon could do this because it is the smallest unit of light that there is and therefore cannot be split in two. This is something which can be tested, and when one sets up the appropriate apparatus to measure whether each photon passes through one or other of the slits or both together, one does find that each photon does go through one or other of the slits, not both.

So, here is the really weird thing. As soon as apparatus is set up to measure which slit each individual photon passes through, the interference stops. However surreptitiously one sneaks a look to see which slit each individual photon passes through, there is no more interference.

Very odd conclusions can be drawn from this. It would appear that light, in the form of photons, passes through one or other of the slits when apparatus is set up specifically to measure which slit it passes through. At the same time, we know that light, in the form of a wave, passes through both slits simultaneously when apparatus is set up to ascertain whether it is a wave by looking for the tell-tale interference pattern. But even individual photons will interfere so long as you do not try to measure which slit they have gone through. It is the act of measuring which decides the outcome.

The above introduces us to a wholly counter-intuitive but fundamental concept in quantum physics, that of the "superposition". The only explanation for the individual photons interfering is that they each went through both slits at the same time, in other words that they were in two different places at the same time. In the words of physics, they were in a superposition, and the mere act of measuring them somehow collapses the superposition so that they return to conventional normality and occupy one position only. Once their superposition is collapsed by measuring them, they are no longer able to be in two places at once, and they can no longer interfere. But leave them alone and do not pry into how they manage their remarkable feat of being in two places at once, and they carry on in their superposition and therefore continue to interfere. There are many other examples of quantum objects being in superpositions, and the consequence of measuring them is always to collapse them. It is as if by taking a peep behind the conjurer's curtain you put him in a sulk, and he refuses to carry on with his magic trick. Except that no matter how hard you look, you never find out how the trick is done.

This leads to another ground-breaking conclusion, which is that it is meaningless to speculate which form the light was in or what it was doing before it was measured, because it is the method used to measure it, and whether it was measured at all, which influences the outcome. This is something which underlies the whole of the quantum world and appears time and time again in this strange place. It is something which many physicists dislike because it means that there are some things which they can never know, and physicists rather like to think that it is possible to know everything. There has been much debate about what is going on at the quantum level to make it so sensitive to being measured. Nothing like this occurs on the macroscopic level that we are used to, where things can be measured and logically understood. It seems that there is a mysterious chasm between the quantum physics which applies to objects in superpositions on the microscopic level, and the classical physics which applies to all the other objects on the macroscopic level.

One of the pioneers of quantum physics was a Danish gentleman called Niels Bohr who, until Hitler invaded his country, used to live in Copenhagen. No doubt after a lot of head-scratching trying to come to some sort of logical understanding of what was the reason for the extraordinary phenomena at the quantum level, he and his fellow thinkers came to the pragmatic conclusion effectively (and I simplify it somewhat) that there is no point in trying to understand the inexplicable. He took the view that until a quantum object has actually been measured it is meaningless to ascribe any reality to it, maybe it does not even exist in any sense that we can understand it. Einstein did not like this idea at all, but the weight of opinion fell behind Bohr, and this became known as the Copenhagen Interpretation.

If in science there are areas where we just have to accept that whatever it is that is going on, it is meaningless to us, then maybe the notion that an all-powerful God would be so far beyond our understanding as to be meaningless would not be a good reason for thinking that such a God would hold no interest for us or that he could not exist. The fact that, because of our own inadequacy, we are not able to comprehend the nature of God should surely not lead us to believe that necessarily he does not exist. What wonders may be found in Copenhagen?

And so, we come to the last fundamental of quantum physics that I want to raise, which is the concept of uncertainty. In our daily lives we are all familiar with the fact that things are uncertain; dare I say with the ever-greater passing of years, ever more so. But the uncertainty which I have in mind is rather more specific. It is known as the Heisenberg uncertainty principle.

I don't think that I need to go into this in detail. It's enough to say that the principle effectively means that on the quantum level, where it is most pronounced, you cannot simultaneously know accurately both the position and the speed of a particle. This means that if you know exactly where it is, you cannot know its exact speed; or if you know its exact speed, you cannot know exactly where it is.

Strictly, the principle states that the product of the uncertainty in an object's momentum (momentum is directly proportional to velocity) and the uncertainty in its position will always be either equal to or greater than a certain fixed amount. Thus, the greater the certainty in the one, the greater will be the uncertainty in the other. The fixed amount is very small, so in our everyday macroscopic lives we are not unduly troubled by Heisenberg. But at the tiny level of quantum objects Heisenberg has a very significant effect. It is not just a question of difficulty in measurement. Heisenberg means that there is a limit to what can be known about quantum objects. It is meaningless (that word again!) to think that a quantum object can ever simultaneously have assigned to it a precise position and a precise momentum.

Perhaps this does not sound very exciting or dramatic. But consider what this would mean if this had proportionately the same effect on the macroscopic level that we are familiar with. It would mean that the driver of the car driving fast, let us say too fast, could never be convicted of speeding. The police might be able to say what his speed was, but they would not be able to say where he was speeding. Maybe he was on a private road where the speed limit would not apply. Or the police could say where he was, but they would have little idea of his speed. The driver himself would be in no better position than the police. It is hard to imagine his state of bewilderment. If we were subject to the weird rules which apply to quantum objects, life as we know it would be impossible.

At the quantum level Heisenberg has other curious effects. A quantum object in a confined space can never be said to be at rest. If it is confined in a precisely known position, then its momentum will always be uncertain.

In fact, Heisenberg is responsible for numerous other relationships between pairs of physical quantities where the same uncertainty applies.

Uncertainty is woven into the very fabric of science at the quantum level. It is inescapable and fundamental. It places an unmovable limit on what can be known.

Drawing all the strands of the above together, Physics shows us that light is a wave, but it is also a stream of particles. If you set out to measure whether light is a wave, you will find that it is a wave. If you set out to measure whether light is a stream of particles, you will find that it is a stream of particles. Those particles can be in two places simultaneously at the same time until you try to measure them, whereupon the act of measuring them immediately causes their 'superposition' to collapse and they return to what we would consider to be normal behaviour.

It is meaningless to speculate which form the light was in, or what it was doing before it was measured, because it is the method used to measure it, and whether it was measured at all, which influences the outcome. Our perception of things depends on how we approach measuring them. This is something which underlies the whole of the quantum world. Arguably until a quantum object has actually been measured it is meaningless to ascribe any reality to it, maybe it does not even exist in any sense that we can understand it, (the Copenhagen Interpretation).

So, we are faced with the reality that there are some things which we just cannot know no matter how hard we try. Unknowable things. And even where we can understand or measure things, there is a limit to the certainty with which we can do it.

CHAPTER THREE

I call to mind a case in which I had to deal with a man who had breached an injunction requiring him not to molest his wife. At that time, we had what I regarded as an excellent system whereby any victim of domestic violence (usually, but not always, a wife or female partner) could come to the County Court and obtain such an injunction. If the police had reasonable cause to suspect that it had been breached they would arrest the perpetrator and bring him before the court the next day. Often the case could be dealt with either straight away or within a very few days, sufficient for the husband to obtain legal representation. Breach of an injunction constituted serious contempt of court and could be dealt with by a prison sentence. Justice was quick and without fuss.

However, in these cases the wife did not necessarily want her husband to be sent to prison. He might lose his job as a result, which could lead to the loss of their home. The children might resent their mother very much for causing their father to be sent to prison. Usually what the wife really wanted was that the husband would stop abusing her. So often the best thing the court could do was to give the man a suspended prison sentence, with a stern warning that if he misbehaved again he would go to prison for the term of the suspended sentence together with any additional sentence for the further transgression.

In this particular case the man's breach of the injunction was such, in my view, as to justify a suspended prison sentence. Having given him the usual dressing down I started to pronounce sentence along the lines: "The sentence of this court is that you shall go to prison for two months …". But before I had a chance to inform him that the sentence would be suspended, he spun round and sprinted out of court like a greyhound out of a trap. Being a county court, there were no police or security to stop him.

I confess that the thought did occur to me that it would serve him right if I did not complete the sentence of suspension. But that would not have been the right thing to do, and I left it to his solicitor to break the good news to him.

That, it seems to me, is a rather fine example of the danger of coming to a conclusion on hearing only half of a story. I'd be willing to bet that a lot of people conclude that God does not exist on hearing only half the story.

So far, I have sought to argue that just because a belief in God may appear to be illogical and too counter-intuitive to be worthy of consideration, that is not a good reason for dismissing it. One cannot escape the fact that things that seem at least as extraordinary as God are part of the bedrock of accepted science. Surely that knowledge must tempt the curiosity of even the most cynical of minds.

So, what then is the evidence for God? The starting point, not surprisingly, has to be the Bible. That usually unopened black book, which in its older versions is full of quaint old English. A book, on the face of it, full of contradictions.

The very existence of the Bible and its contents is enough for some people to be convinced of God's existence. For many, however, the Bible is not self-proving.

The Bible is in two basic sections, the Old Testament and the New Testament. The Old Testament consists of thirty-nine books dealing with the history of the Jews, including their many tribulations, their laws and the development of their religious beliefs. The New Testament consists of twenty-seven books, dealing with the birth, life, death and resurrection of Jesus Christ and subsequent events, including the thoughts and deeds of the early Christians. My understanding is that altogether the Bible was written by forty or more different authors over a period of one thousand five hundred years or more. The authors included kings, fishermen, poets, scholars, historians and doctors. Unsurprisingly there are indeed many contradictions. Sadly, there have been and remain huge arguments between theologians and ministers and even their congregations about their various interpretations of the Bible and how the practice of Christianity should best be pursued. Regrettably any respectably comprehensive analysis of the Bible would be totally beyond the capacity of this short book and indeed the capability of its author. The best that I can do is explain my view of things and what has had the most influence on me.

All serious scholars do, I think, accept that Jesus did exist and that he was executed by crucifixion. Independently of the Bible, there are references to him and his crucifixion in Roman texts, and the Romans would be unlikely to have had any interest in inventing such a person. What theologians and others seem to disagree about is to do with the who, what, why, how and anything else they can think of to argue about over Jesus. So, it is hardly surprising that people who are not particularly interested in the subject anyway look at the occasional newspaper headlines highlighting the latest conflicting view and switch off. Yes, maybe Jesus did exist and was a good man, but so what? Why should I believe in all the crazy miraculous stuff when even the experts and ordinary Christians cannot agree?

For me, the most fruitful places to look in the Bible are the four gospels: Matthew, Mark, Luke and John. With considerable trepidation I will attempt to summarise their fundamental message as saying that about two thousand years ago Jesus was born by immaculate conception; that, even as a child, he showed a remarkable understanding of the Jewish religion; that he worked for most of his life as a carpenter; and then at the age of about thirty embarked on a mission to explain the true nature of God (often in conflict with his Jewish religion) performing numerous miracles as he did so. After about three years of upsetting the religious scholars and theologians of his day he was crucified at their behest. On the third day after having died on the cross, he was resurrected back to life, appeared to many witnesses over a period of several weeks, and then vanished from sight.

What one draws from reading the gospels is that Jesus was clearly saying that God does exist. Moreover, and hugely importantly, that this is an all-powerful God who created the Universe, and us, and who provides us with freedom of will and with life after death. This is a God of infinite love and compassion. If Jesus was indeed what the gospels say he was, as a sort of shorthand the son of God with divine knowledge of God, then that God does exist. The question is: to what extent, if at all, can one rely upon the veracity of the gospels?

The initial appraisal of the case for the gospels does not appear to look particularly good. The first gospel to be written was probably that of Mark, and it was not written until about forty years after Jesus' crucifixion. There is considerable scholarly debate about the provenance of the gospels and to what extent they were written, or caused to be written, by people who had actually witnessed the events of which they tell. It is thought that Mark may have come across Jesus at least occasionally. Certainly, this gospel is not a contemporaneous account of those events. It may be to some extent a compilation of some of the many memories which his disciples recounted of Jesus, and with which Mark would have been very familiar.

The gospels of Matthew and Luke were written after Mark, and both copied numerous extracts from Mark as well as adding other material, possibly garnered from further oral recollections, not to be found in Mark.

John's gospel is perhaps the most insightful. Until recently, the received wisdom was that John's gospel was not a first-hand account either, but now there are strong arguments that it is. It is rather different to the other three, and it provides a deeper interpretation of the significance of the events in question.

So why should one give the gospels any credence, written, as they were, decades after the events of which they speak by people who mostly did not witness those events themselves? Gospels which were probably written with more of an intention to spread the good news of Christianity than with an intention to set down an accurate historical record. Are they an elaborate and bizarre hoax, or perhaps just a fantasy of wishful thinking?

It would be curious if they were either of those things. The Jews had for many centuries been expecting a messiah, as foretold in the old testament. Jesus had himself said that he was that messiah. However, the messiah the Jews expected was a powerful king who would deliver them from their various woes and do all manner of good for them. If the early Christians were going to invent the messiah on which the gospels were based then why would they invent one who was the complete opposite of what was expected, someone who was born into poverty in a stable and who was executed as a criminal on a cross? Someone who did nothing for the Jews, who even challenged many of their beliefs. Why invent a story that no one was likely to believe?

More specifically, why would they themselves believe, if they did, that the Jesus who had in his lifetime stoked up expectations of glory and then dashed them by his inglorious and powerless death in agony on a cross be such a messiah? On the face of it he was a total failure. Unless, of course, that had not been the end of it. Unless they really believed that he had been resurrected, that he had performed the supreme miracle and beaten death. That would change everything.

It is possible that such a belief could have been genuinely held, but not necessarily based on fact. So, is there any evidence to suppose that the incredible story of the resurrection was true?

Some two thousand years after the event there can obviously be no direct evidence. But one can draw inferences from what happened after Jesus' crucifixion. In its immediate aftermath, Jesus' disciples and other followers must have been hopelessly disillusioned and beset by grief, all their high hopes devastated. In addition to that, they must have been fearful that as Jesus' followers they might be in for the same fate as him. Yet as stated elsewhere in the new testament, and as must have been the case, within a few weeks these same disciples were courageously defying the authorities and preaching to large crowds of the resurrection of Jesus, the messiah. I say that this must have been the case because according to the experts, by about the time that Mark wrote his gospel, that is to say by about forty years after the crucifixion, numerous people had been converted to Christianity and Christian churches had been set up in Palestine, Syria, Asia Minor, Egypt, Greece and Italy. That was a remarkable achievement in those brutal times, and I cannot think that it would have been likely to have been brought about by those early endangered proselytisers unless they had actually witnessed and been emboldened and inspired by something truly exceptional. Self-deception would hardly come close to that.

Something must have rocketed Jesus' disciples from the crushing defeat of Jesus' death on the cross to the fearless and inspired men who travelled far and wide to spread the news of Christianity to all who would listen regardless of the consequences. Those consequences were often that they also suffered torture and execution themselves. It is a difficult exercise to grope back two thousand years into the past. The evidence is not as good as ideally one would like. But one must deal as best one can with what has come down to us from that time. Crucially, as I have attempted to demonstrate earlier, it may be unwise to shut out anything just because it may logically or intuitively appear to be impossible. If one is forced into making a decision, it seems to me more likely than not that what the Bible says about the resurrection is true, miraculous as it may have been, and that without the resurrection Christianity would have ended in bloody misery hanging on three nails on a cross two thousand years ago.

If one does accept that what one might regard as the most extraordinary part of the gospels is true, namely that the resurrection did take place, then it must follow that it would be reasonable to accept that the rest of the gospels is probably true also. That brings me back to my earlier assertion that if what the gospels say about Jesus is true, then his teachings about God were true.

Although it is not the purpose of this book to go into the details of Christianity, I should say in passing that aside from the resurrection, the contents of the gospels do, for me, reinforce the genuineness of Jesus. His teachings seem to me to be self-evidently correct, albeit his strictures for the likes of me largely aspirational. Since I am the product of my upbringing and culture, one might say that that is only to be expected. But two thousand years ago, his teachings must have been revelatory. How would a low born carpenter have achieved that unless there was something extraordinary about him? In those harsh and violent times, he took those who listened to him into what must have been very unfamiliar territory. I give four examples which may be familiar to many people: Firstly, He defined our neighbour, effectively, as anyone who needs our help. Secondly, *Blessed are the peacemakers.* Thirdly, *Let he who is without sin cast the first stone.* Fourthly, He urged that there is no point in worrying, it gets you nowhere. Most people would now agree that all that is self-evident. But in those days, to minds rigid with doctrine and tradition, it must have been ground-breaking. Christians would say that he was a man who had reason to know what he was talking about.

Some people will point to the inconsistencies in the Bible and argue that they discredit and undermine the whole thing. How can an eye for an eye and a tooth for a tooth coexist with turning the other cheek and loving your neighbour? But that precisely exemplifies what Jesus was all about. His message was that those cruel inflexible doctrines of the old religious beliefs were wrong, so of course his teaching conflicted with much of what had gone before. When one considers that the majority of the Bible was written over many centuries by numerous different people, long before Jesus came along, all groping for an understanding of God that was way beyond their ability, then one can see that contradictions were inevitable. But Christians do need the old testament fully to understand many of the references which Jesus made and the background and beliefs of the people of the time to whom he preached. He needed to talk to them in terms that they understood. And for those of us who question why, if Jesus was the son of God, it was necessary for him to suffer such a monstrously cruel death, the answer must be that crucifixion was a standard Roman method of execution in those days. Something which the people of the time also understood.

So that, in a nutshell, is my understanding of Christianity.

Apart from the culture which I grew up in and the Bible, there is another source of my belief: it comes from my personal experiences.

I appreciate that my personal experiences will probably mean little to you. They may seem to you to be banal and of no significance. And yet to me they are probably the most important things of all. Such experiences have taken various forms and are hard to define, but mostly they involved some sort of coincidence or series of closely connected coincidences. Usually, they consisted of me having a particular thought or concern or question in mind, to be followed by something happening external to myself which chimed exactly with what was in my mind and which answered my question or concern. To give a flavour of them, I will set out a selection of these experiences below.

THE FIRST

We go back to a week in mid-March 1994. I was then in practice as a solicitor, and on each day of that week something unexpected but good had occurred. The details are now a little hazy, but it went along these lines.

On the Monday I received payment for a legal aid case in which I had acted for a woman who had presumably not greatly cared for the advice I gave her and who had transferred her affections to another firm of solicitors so many years before that I had completely forgotten about it. It was not a large payment, but it was nice to get it.

On the Tuesday, having received a rather pessimistic advice from counsel on the merits of pursuing a case on behalf of a man suffering from vibration white finger, and facing the possibility of having his legal aid discharged, I telephoned the other side and rather to my surprise managed to persuade them to settle on a full liability basis.

On the Wednesday something similar happened, but I cannot remember what it was.

On the Thursday I was served with the defendant's expert pilot's report in a fatal air-crash case in which I was acting for some of the dependants of the victims. The case was due to go to trial a few weeks later. Normally the receipt of the other side's expert report, if it is a good one, would tend to give rise to at least a few misgivings and not a little gloom. But this one was so weak that it was immediately clear that if the trial judge were to have at least a smattering of technical understanding then we really should win. For months, this case had been taking up nearly all my time to prepare, and this report, which should have been like an Exocet missile fired into our bows, was actually an absolute gift, and meant that my own flying expert's evidence would effectively meet with no credible challenge.

And then, the Friday. This was when the first of my unusual experiences happened. I had come home from the office early because my wife Helen and son Tom and I were going to the theatre to see what turned out to be a rather un-engaging modern dress version of, I think, Macbeth. As I walked into the kitchen I saw on the table in its distinctive envelope my payslip from the Lord Chancellor's Department for my previous months' deputy district judge sittings. I knew how many days I had sat and exactly how much was due to be paid. Unlike the previous four days, nothing particularly good had happened in the office that Friday. I suppose that I must have been going through a bit of a cosying-up to God phase in my life, and somewhat flippantly I said, "Okay God, so then, is today's good thing to be a bonus from the Lord Chancellor?"

Now, the Lord Chancellor, Lord Mackay, was a very fine and honourable man with a huge Scottish gravitas, but it is, I think, fair to say that he was not renowned for making frivolous and unnecessary payments to anyone. For all his virtues, the notion of him or his department paying me a bonus was absurd.

I opened the envelope, and, as you will have guessed, it enclosed a rather larger payment than I had calculated I was entitled to. It was not actually a bonus, but it included a payment for half a day more than I had sat in the Harlow County Court.

I telephoned the Lord Chancellor's Department to ask how they would like me to return the excess payment, but they told me that

I was entitled to keep it because although I had only sat for the half day in question, I had originally been booked for the whole day and therefore that was what they had to pay me for. They seemed horrified at the prospect of any money being returned to them; I don't think that they had any procedure for that sort of thing.

It was not a huge sum, but I am sure that it was the closest that Lord Mackay ever came to paying a bonus, or anything like it, to anyone.

I suppose that at the time I must have been a bit ambivalent about whether the Almighty was really communicating with me in some curious way. Why would he? Why in all his almightiness would he be going to all that trouble over such a relatively small amount of money, such a little thing? Indeed, over me? And yet, it was undeniable that following all the other events that week I had, albeit light-heartedly, made that impudent challenge to God. I had not for one moment expected any sort of response. But in its own way the challenge seemed to have been answered, instantly. Clearly it was not the amount that was important. What mattered was that something had been communicated to me, although I couldn't understand what it was. Unless, of course, it was just a rather extraordinary coincidence.

I expect that if nothing else had happened I would have thought no more about it and put it down to one of life's weird coincidences. But it was only the start.

THE SECOND

The next day, the Saturday, I set off with our dog Denning on a walk; Denning, as always, enthusiastically bounding ahead when let off the lead. As I walked down the track towards the nearby spinney I heard what I can best describe as a little voice in my head. It was not as if someone had spoken directly to me, it was more like the memory of a voice when someone has said a sentence to which you have not paid attention, but then suddenly you realise that you want to know what it was and if you are quick enough you can hear it repeat in your mind. I cannot remember the exact words, but it effectively said this:

"Today the best thing of all the week will happen."

Perhaps strangely, I don't think that I was at all surprised to hear a voice in my head. A psychiatrist may suggest that it was a sign of schizophrenia, but I don't think that it was. What did surprise me was what it said. The postman had come earlier, so there could be no unexpected good news. It seemed highly improbable that the voice could be right.

I continued with the walk, taking a different route to normal. Down by the double reservoirs I crossed the brook and turned right towards the ford. Then I came back, walking up the nearby farmer's field to the track which runs from his field along to the trees where the bluebells grow amongst the fox holes. As I walked along the track, Denning suddenly shot off ahead in the determined sort of way which he reserved for sightings of things which interested him, such as rabbits and pheasants and people. To my discomfort, for it was a muddy walk and I knew what he had in mind, I saw that on this occasion it was a person. In the distance I could see a figure standing by the gate to the field where we once went sledging. My shouted efforts to restrain Denning were futile. He continued to race towards the unfortunate soon to be mud-splattered person. I quickened my pace. As I came closer, rehearsing my apologies, I saw Denning do his predicted leap up against the person's legs. Simultaneously, and to my great and surprised relief, I could see now that this was no stranger, but Tom. Denning's delight was exceeded only by my own.

I say surprised, because at that stage fourteen-year-old Tom was not the keenest of walkers. I am not sure that he had ever voluntarily gone off for a walk on his own before. But there he was. He had guessed where he might meet me, and he had come to meet me. And then I realised that the little voice had been right. This was by far the best thing that had happened all week. To have such a lovely son abandon all the other things which he would normally have preferred to do and come out to meet me – what could be better than that? I felt deeply privileged.

In our conversation on the way home, Tom told me how he had waited at the gate for quite a while hoping to see me, and had been on the point of giving up, when Denning and I came into view. Had I been any later I would have missed him, and had I not taken a detour and been earlier we would not have had much of a walk back together. He had waited at the best possible place and time.

Others might see this as only a little thing, nothing special. The sort of thing that happens all the time in families. No doubt it does. But not so common when first predicted by a little voice in one's head. A voice which now moved me to my heart.

THE THIRD

Thursday 31st March 1994 was the day before Good Friday. It had been a normal day in the office, though the stress of the air crash case was building up with the trial only five weeks away. Despite the weakness of the other side's flying expert's report, and subsequently the receipt of a less important but equally weak radar expert's report, I could never be sure that I hadn't overlooked something, or that the other side didn't have some sort of bombshell up their sleeve.

At about four thirty p.m. as I sat at my desk a pain began to build up in my chest. I'd had chest pains before, but nothing like as intense as this became. It was bad enough to stop me doing any work, I couldn't concentrate on anything apart from my discomfort. Inevitably I wondered whether it was the start of a heart attack, and, as one does, I engaged in some rather urgent prayers asking to be spared a little longer, at least until the children had fully grown up.

On reflection, I think that it must have been a particularly unpleasant bout of reflux. Whatever it was, it was over by about five p.m.. My lovely secretary Gill brought me a coffee, I may have had a cigarette, and all was well.

Because it was the Easter weekend my niece Madeline was staying with us, and my daughter Katherine and son Tom were both at home. Helen had prepared baked potatoes for supper. As she took them out of the oven she put on my plate a potato which had the exact shape of a heart, or at least the accepted pictorial shape of a heart. I asked her when she had chosen it from the sack. It transpired that she had done this at the same time that I had thought that I might be having the heart attack, saying those prayers. Being the romantic she is, she told me that she had selected it specially for me.

It could have been coincidence, of course. But I had little doubt that it was a graphic answer to those prayers. Quite what the answer meant I did not know.

THE INTERPRETATION

I cannot remember how long it took me to work it out; no more than two weeks I think. From time to time, I pondered upon what it all meant. I felt pretty sure that it had to mean something. Then, one afternoon as I was walking down towards the brook by the lower meadow it suddenly came to me all at once. Each of my three experiences had concerned the things that I was worrying about the most, in order of priority.

The first experience had concerned finance. In early 1994 my firm's finances had been difficult and getting worse, in common I believe with many other firms of solicitors and businesses generally at that time. The situation was dire. It was an enormous anxiety. The realisation hit me that it was not the extra half day's pay for sitting in Harlow that was important. It was the overall subject matter of the experience, namely finance.

The second concerned my family, as represented by Tom. I was always worrying to some extent about the comings and goings of Helen and the children, and here we had an unusual little journey by Tom to come to meet me, my joy over which had somehow been foretold to me in advance.

The third concerned my health, or rather safety. In those days I had a private pilot's licence and used to go flying every month. In the cold grey hours of any dawn before a flight I was growing ever more open to the idea that things might go badly wrong, resulting in me not being there for my family. It was not the thought of dying which troubled me so much, although I didn't particularly want to die, it was the thought of being separated from Helen, Katherine and Tom. The more experienced and – I hope, proficient – I became at flying, the more I worried about it, although as soon as I would actually get into the cockpit all the trepidation would disappear and I would enjoy the flight. I suppose it was acting in the air crash case, knowing that the pilot had been vastly more experienced than me but that, even so, he had made a most fundamental mistake, and remembering the photographs of the wreckage containing the crumpled burnt bodies of the victims, one of whom I had known quite well, that brought the dangers home to me.

So, what did it all mean? Three pairs of curious but in themselves not very important coincidences. A little extra unexpected money from the Lord Chancellor's Department; Tom going on an unexpected and unusual walk to meet me; and a heart attack that wasn't. I realised that the importance was in the delivery of the messages rather than the specific contents. I understood it to mean, and still do, that God had complete knowledge of and interest in what I was doing and thinking. That He had arranged events or come into my thoughts in such a way as to give me that understanding, and more importantly that the future would turn out in such a way that I had no need to worry. That it was all in his Hands. He had delivered them with a kindly and slightly zany sense of humour as perhaps befitted a silly man worrying unnecessarily. What better for a man who had survived and prayed over a heart attack (that was really indigestion) than to give him a heart-shaped baked potato?

Those first three events seemed to fit together to form one simple message. The following two were rather more free standing.

THE FOURTH

Saturday 18th June 1994 was an idyllic Summer's day. I set off for a walk after lunch as usual. The sky was cloudless blue and the temperature beautifully warm but not too hot. The firm's finances had turned around and come good. All was well with the family. Everything was perfect. But I was confused.

I had always assumed that God did not interfere with our lives, save perhaps exceptionally for miracles and maybe sometimes answers to prayers. I had thought that our chances in life were random, and that in that way we all have such freedom of will as is not curtailed or shaped by our circumstances or by others exercising their freedom of will. But here I was on this lovely Summer's day, having had the extraordinary privilege of God having communicated with me three times, and His first communication not to worry about money having already turned out to be munificently correct. Why, I wondered, should I be so incredibly fortunate? Surely the system wasn't supposed to work like this. God did not interfere or manipulate. What was going on?

I walked a long way that balmy afternoon. Up through our nearby farmer's fields in the direction of what we called the spooky farm, then right by a lonely cottage and down towards the village of Shalford. The big field on the way to Shalford was full of oil seed rape in bright yellow flower, peppered with luscious red poppies flopping lazily in the gentle breeze. Down at the bottom before reaching Shalford I turned right into a cool undulating wood I had never been into before. Then I retraced my steps back up to the cottage at the top and turned left onto the bridleway back towards the farm.

As I was walking along the bridleway, full of contentment, I heard that little voice in my head again. It was just like it had been three months earlier when I had set out on the walk on which Tom had come to meet me. I wasn't surprised to hear it, although I had certainly not expected it. Perhaps on such a heavenly afternoon it seemed only natural.

It said, "Look up. What do you see?"

I had been looking down on the ground ahead of me, and I duly looked up and likewise in my head replied, "A path."

"How did the path get there?" the voice asked.

I took some time to think about that. My thoughts were my reply. I realised that originally the position of the path would have been governed by the topography of the land, how the glaciers which I knew to have been there long ago had cut and shaped it. Then, over the more recent millennia, the position of the path would have been governed by the needs of the hundreds of generations living in the vicinity. Maybe there had been some influence from Roman settlements, Anglo Saxon villages, neighbouring farms and so on. Over the millennia all those needs and influences had brought about where it was, and what it was. There had been no need for a six-lane motorway here, nor even a single-track road. Everything had come together to mould it as the bridleway it was.

As I finished my train of thought the voice pressed further. "Why are you travelling on the path?"

"Because I know it takes me home." Even as I formulated my reply, I realised that the question had not been as facile as it seemed. The path was not straight, there were several twists and turns in it, and it wandered a good way off from a straight line from where I was to home. There were hedges and fences which would have prevented me from taking such a straight line. Though it would not have been obvious to someone unfamiliar with the area, I knew it was the best way home.

"Then consider it to be like your path through life."

I don't think it took long for the reply to sink in. I had the answer to my earlier puzzlement. God had his own way of doing things which did not interfere with randomness and freedom of will. Numerous generations of people, all exercising their individual freedom of will, had between them created the path on which I had chosen to be walking. And in much the same way, in my lifetime in all my many and random interactions with all the people I had and would come across, all of them exercising their own freedom of will, there would be the right path for me to take if I so chose. An all-powerful, all-knowing God did not need to manipulate or control what people did. To bring about his will in me he had only to navigate a path for me to follow and, I suppose, hope that I would exercise my free will to follow it. The same would apply to anyone else.

My lovely summer afternoon revelation did not explain why I was being so favoured, in particular by being given such revelations. But it was such a huge and unexpected insight into one of the ways that God works that it was more than enough to keep me going. It was quite a comfort to understand that there was a path for me to follow, as long as I made the right decisions about following it. Now, on reflection, I see that it perhaps raises more questions than answers. But as I look back, I hope that by and large I have made the right decisions, though of course there must always be the doubt that I have not. And now, in retirement, I wonder how far and where else that path may lead.

THE FITH

Now we come, just over a week later, to Sunday 26th June 1994. It was the day of the village fête. In the evening Helen, Katherine and Tom all went up there for some sort of hot dog supper, while I, never having been that keen on communal gatherings, stayed at home.

As I sat finishing rather greedily some cheese and biscuits, I saw that a glorious sunset was happening outside. Taking a last glass of wine with me, I went outside to view it properly. As I stood on the terrace looking towards the West, the little voice again appeared in my head.

"Look up," it said.

There was a lot of sky to look up at, but I seemed to know exactly which part of it the voice meant. High up above me was a thin broken layer of cumulus cloud, and in the middle of it a hole was hollowed out with light blue sky showing through. The hole was in the exact pictorial shape of a heart. It lay on its side, with the pointed end facing towards the North West. I realised straight away that this was another of those communications. The connection with the heart-shaped potato was unmistakable. But I was rather surprised, and I think a little disappointed to see that a vapour trail from a by now disappeared aircraft ran horizontally right through the centre of it, from the dimpled end on the left through the pointed end on the right. I remember wondering why God had gone to all the trouble of creating for me such a display in the sky, only to have it spoilt by a vapour trail.

As I was thinking about it, my thoughts perhaps a little dulled by the wine, the little voice in my head said, "Follow the vapour trail."

Which I did. Swivelling my eyes to the right along the vapour trail I saw that it led to the loveliest and brightest part of the sunset. And then I understood what it meant. The heart of course is the symbol of love. The lightest part of the sky I took to represent 'The Light, or God'. If this was a message from God, which I believed then and still do, it was 'love me'.

Of course, even from my not very extensive reading of the Bible I must have come across this commandment to love God before. Probably lots of times. I am sorry to say that it had never made much impression on me. I suppose that I had never understood how one might follow it, and therefore never really tried either to follow it or even bestow on it the importance of remembering it. So it came as a bit of a shock to me a few weeks later when reading a book about some famous people's favourite religious texts to see that this was actually God's first and greatest commandment.

Having been treated to my own personal rendition, I began to think for the first time that I ought to begin to take it seriously and try to follow it. I suppose God thought that I was so dim that that was the only way he might kick-start me into doing so.

For the next few months, mostly on weekend walks in the countryside, I pondered upon these experiences. Why, I wondered, had I been given such extraordinary privileges? Unless, of course, they were not, and I had naively deluded myself about the element of God. Perhaps after all they were just very weird coincidences, and I had imagined into them more than they deserved. But there was no doubt that they had happened, including in three of them that little voice in my head. Psychiatrists and most other people might say that little voices in the head means madness, but I didn't think I was mad or that there was any other evidence that I was, and a delusional little voice would hardly be predictive as this one had been on a couple of the occasions. I could not have known beforehand that Tom would untypically come to meet me on the walk, nor that there would be the shape of a heart in the clouds when I followed the instruction to look up. In any event, two of the experiences had not involved any little voice at all. One might have thought that had I embarked upon some sort of schizophrenic episode then the little voice would have been present in all of them.

Furthermore, my five experiences seemed to connect together so neatly and cleverly. Each reinforced the others. Though each one had a different format, they were all of a kind. The more I analysed them the more convinced I became that, much more probably than not, my perception and understanding of them was correct.

Which in the first instance meant that I really ought to get to work on the last one. Quite why God would be concerned about me loving him I didn't know, but it seemed that that was what he wanted. But how was I to do that when I really didn't know what he was like? How do you love someone or something that you can't even begin to visualise?

The autumn of 1994 was particularly beautiful. The colours of the leaves were spectacular, fabulous in the sunshine. One bright autumn afternoon as I walked through the lower meadow looking up at the glorious trees I was wondering about the answers to those questions when there popped into my head something which I think must be in the Bible somewhere. Not the little voice this time, but something I remembered:

'By my works you shall know me'.

That was not a complete answer, but it was a clue. The intricate beauty of the millions of leaves was surely a wonderful gift, as were all the other good and happy things in my life. Surely a Being who bestowed such gifts had to be lovable. More than that, surely such generosity must imply that such a Being was full of love for me, inexplicable as that might be. However incapable I was of visualising or comprehending him, such love seemed naturally to demand reciprocation.

But my recalcitrance was not done yet. How, I wondered, could I love someone or something one cannot be sure exists? I continued the walk and crossed over Pod's brook near the reservoirs and stood for a while in the trees on the other side.

Then another thought popped into my head. 'How could God be any less real than his creation?'

For as long as I can remember I had always assumed, whenever I turned my mind to such things, that God had created the universe and everything in it. I had been brought up to believe that, and that view had been supported by my albeit fleeting and uncritical understanding of the Bible derived from childhood scripture lessons and so forth. More than that, it had always seemed to me to be incomprehensible that the universe had come into existence on its own. Therefore, it had needed God to create it. I had always accepted that I was too lowly a being to be able to understand the answers to the questions that raised, and I had been content to leave it at that.

I still did believe that God had created everything, but now I could see what that meant. God could not be any less real than his creation. He was as real as the ground on which I stood, the trees round about me; all that I knew, and every truth that could ever be known about science and mathematics. There could be no half measures, half beliefs. If God had brought about creation, he was as real as everything else in life.

So that is pretty much the package of stuff which has brought me to where I am now. The sceptic would point out that coincidences and strange experiences do happen all the time, and of course they do. Mostly they are insignificant. The difference here is the element of what had been in my mind. That is what makes it meaningful to me. The sceptic would accuse me of self-induced gullibility. Maybe so. And maybe not. I am the only one who can say precisely what was in my mind, and why the experience was one, for me, beyond the bounds of the commonplace.

I have heard of others who have had similar experiences; for some, they have been life changing. I and they have little doubt that they have come from an external and divine source. I know that it sounds hugely presumptuous for me to suggest that any divine source would have any interest in communicating with me. But I do not know the mind of God, and having gone to the trouble of creating me, perhaps he wants a little word with me from time to time. Perhaps he wants me to do things that I would not otherwise do, like writing this book. The important word is *perhaps*. If I and others are to retain our freedom of will then we must be allowed to choose whether or not to believe in such communications; whether or not to be receptive to them. If God were to speak to me with a voice of thunder in such a way that I knew for sure that it was him, then, apart from scaring the living daylights out of me, I would know that I had no choice but to do as he asked. That, it seems, is fortunately not how he operates.

Therein, perhaps, lies another point. As I mentioned earlier, in certain experiments in quantum physics what you measure depends on how you set up the apparatus you use to measure it.

The very act of measuring can determine the thing being measured. Maybe by analogy one will only understand a divine communication if one is receptive to it, and without that receptiveness the communication will pass by unnoticed or meaningless. When the measuring apparatus is to be found in a laboratory the results are not likely to be criticised just because they are weird and counter intuitive. But tell a sceptic that perhaps you have had a divine communication and he will think you are stupid or mad.

Some people will say that they are absolutely certain that God, perhaps I should say that *their* God, exists. They have no doubt. There is nothing wrong with that. Perhaps they have had experiences which I have not. What can trouble me about that, however, is that sometimes they have equally trenchant convictions about the nature of God. For some people he is somewhat stern and unforgiving. I hope they are wrong. That is not my understanding of God from the gospels. Nor, I think, was it Jesus' understanding. We read in the account of his crucifixion that shortly before his death he cried out those agonised words: *My God, my God, why have you forsaken me?* Clearly his belief in God was still rock solid, but perhaps here we have a suggestion that even Jesus did not know all the answers.

For my part, I am happy to accept that my simple mind is incapable of encompassing the vastness of God. The best description for me is that God is love. I don't think that it is necessary to approach him through esoteric ceremonies or gold tapestried vestments. That helps for some people and that's fine, though I tend to think that it may put some other people off the whole idea.

A God of love and compassion, you may query, with this world full of cruelty and suffering? How could such a God allow Hitler and Stalin and all the other monsters of past and present to inflict such misery upon mankind? The answer that everyone has freedom of will to do as much good or evil as they like clearly is not much of an explanation. What about their victims' freedom of will to live their lives in peace and happiness? How could God apparently have such contradictory faces? Human logic would calculate that such a thing is not possible, and therefore that no such God exists. But as we see from quantum physics, human logic may not be a reliable guide when applied to concepts far beyond our understanding.

You may still feel it is most unlikely, if there is a God who created the universe and in particular humankind, that he would seemingly have made such a mess of it. Surely a God of love and compassion would have given us such certainty of his existence and how we should conduct our lives and our dealings with one another that we would never have to experience the numerous and dreadful miseries that we inflict on one another. Why would such a God not have given us that comfortable certainty that science is perceived as giving us? But as we see from Heisenberg's Uncertainty Principle, science does not give us certainty at the quantum level. Why, when uncertainty is part of our natural world, should we expect certainty about God?

But in any event, you may ask, if God does exist, why does he not give us proof of his existence?

The answer to that, it seems to me, must be that if God does exist then he does not want us to have that proof. Perhaps that is a simple answer for a simple man, but one can see the logic of it. If we are to have freedom of will, albeit buffeted and curtailed as our individual freedom of will is by the exercise by others of their freedom of will, then our freedom of will has to be free from any compulsion from God. If we knew for absolute certain that God does exist and what he expects of us then most of us, I suspect, would follow like sheep. For practical purposes our freedom of will would be a chimera. Life would be a pointless exercise in doing what we are told, rather like the unfortunate inhabitants of a totalitarian state. For it to work, freedom of will must surely include the freedom to believe or not to believe in whatever we want to, including the existence of God. That is why believers have to make do with faith, that curious state of mind which believes things to be true without proof. As with quantum physics, it seems that some uncertainty in this aspect of our lives is part of the package.

It then follows that we must accept that it is unlikely that we are ever going to have absolute proof of God's existence. To demand such a high standard of proof before entertaining the possibility of God's existence is surely unreasonable. So what standard of proof would it be reasonable to apply? Should it be beyond a reasonable doubt? I don't think so. God either exists or he does not. One thing or the other. If the question were being decided in a civil court the judge would decide the issue on the balance of probabilities. He or she would have to decide whether God's existence was more likely than not. If one could reduce it to numbers, fifty-one to forty-nine percent would swing it in God's favour, and vice versa.

I suspect that most people's instinct would be to set the bar rather higher than that, but I do not see any logical reason why one should, any more than would the judge in a civil trial. God either exists, or he does not. Why should the test be set higher for one side, and lower for the other? However, each to his or her own.

It is easy to focus on the negative aspects of life and conclude that no loving God could have created this world of so many sorrows. But I think that we should not forget all the truly wonderful things that are woven into our existence. Not for everyone, I know. Tragically, this is not a fair world. But if we choose to ignore the good things or deny them to others then it is difficult to see how God can do much about that if freedom of will is to be preserved. But who would deny the beauty of this world, from the glory of towering mountain ranges to the gentle loveliness of perfumed flowers, the selfless love of most parents for their children and the kindliness of so many people for others whom they scarcely know? And whilst we are at it, who can deny the wonder of life itself, of our own lives? In all these things and so many more we can see, if we look, the glory of God. I would suggest that for most of us, certainly in western society, the good far outweighs the bad. If it was God who set us down where we find ourselves to be, should we not look first at our own surroundings when considering whether he exists? Yes, there are sorrows, but there is also great happiness and joy surely reflecting the love that God has for us. Is it really more likely that all those complex emotions are just the random result of the interactions of the chemicals which make up our bodies?

Does God really matter, you may ask? If God is as I described him at the beginning, then resoundingly the answer must surely be yes. That is to say the God as I understand him from his description in the gospels, an all-powerful God of love and compassion, who created the universe, and us, and who provides us with freedom of will and life after death.

I know that the existence of God raises as many questions as it answers, not least of which is where did God come from? My only answer to that is remember Copenhagen and get on with life. It is of course up to each individual to decide whether he or she considers whether God probably does or does not exist. If your conclusion is no, so be it. But at least you can hold the door open to that possibility, and it may be that in due course something will happen to make you reconsider.

If your decision is yes, you may still have lots of questions. But you will have a lot of answers too. You will know that the four billion years spanning the formation of this planet and evolution to produce you have achieved more than a meaningless transitory little spark of life, but a life which has a purpose and a meaning. You will know that that life and the lives of those you love will not snuff out on death. That I hope will be a comfort to you. Perhaps not so comfortable, though, as you realise that you may meet again beyond the grave any people whom you have wronged in this life.

If you read the Bible, in particular the new testament, you will find a simple guide as to how best to lead your life. I think that guide is a great deal less cluttered up than some people seem to believe. You may even like to try talking to God – you don't have to wait until some dark time in your life engulfs you before you do that. Maybe you will get some answers if you are receptive enough to look out for them, but perhaps not in a form you would ever expect.

Most important of all, you will know (if you don't know already) that it is love which makes your life worthwhile, even if the only love for you is that from God. You will know that it is love which underpins everything worthwhile, and which is ultimately the only hope for our broken world.

My purpose in writing this little book is to help people at least to consider that it is realistic to hope that there is life after death. For me, the thought that I and my loved ones would simply snuff out on death would be profoundly depressing. What dreadful finality, and what an egregious waste of all that a lifetime's experience and knowledge and wisdom and love has crafted within us. As I have indicated, my belief that there is life after death is inextricably linked to my belief in the existence of God, whose message through Jesus was that there is, and without whom I don't think that it would be possible. That is why, unqualified as I am, I have spent some time dealing with the question of the existence of God.

Never having been dead, I do not know precisely what awaits us. As I understand it, we will carry on just as we are (or were before any dementia or other ill health may have afflicted us) but without our physical bodies. We will look the same and be the same. I do not think that we will lounge around on clouds, nor do I think that we will be sent to any such place as hell. Hell may be our true realisation of any hurt we have done to others. I suspect that we will be as busy after death as before. The big differences will be that we will be freed from the physical needs and restraints of our human bodies, and we will then know for sure about God. We will have a new understanding of things just as in the past we have had fundamental new understandings of our existence on earth brought about by discoveries in science.

As the Bible puts it: *And God shall wipe away all tears from their eyes; and there shall be no more death, neither sorrow, nor crying, neither shall there be any more pain: for the former things are passed away.*

If, nonetheless, you feel so confident that your knowledge of this weird, mysterious existence of ours is so profound that you can be certain that there is no God, no life after death, no hope, then I stand back in awe at the immensity of your faith. For faith is all that it will be. Scepticism is not proof. You will have no proof, any more than I have proof of my beliefs.

Still, I would ask you to continue to consider it, to lend your mind to the possibility that if you were to be receptive to concepts beyond comfortable familiarity and earthly logic, then you may find truths that will surprise you. You may then find the hope that I urge upon you. When the time comes, I hope that you do.

ACKNOWLEDGMENTS

My huge thanks to everyone who has helped me to put this book together, in particular to:

Dr. Sugi Furuta

The Revd. Tim Goodbody

My lovely, patient wife and children, Helen, Katherine and Tom, especially to Katherine who unstintingly gave her time and skills to mould it into shape.

The author

Philip Pelly was born in 1948, and grew up in Wiltshire. He studied Physics at the University of London before teaching for two years. He then qualified as a solicitor and went on to become a district judge. He is married to Helen, a priest in the Church of England. They have two children and three grandchildren. He loves the coast, walking and wine. This is his first book.